The Adventure Begins

_____

_____

My Cruise Trip Daily Agenda

PAGE	DAY	ACTIVITIES	PLACE	DATE

Today's Plans:

_____

_____

Cruise Day #_____

Date: ___/___/___

Places:

Weather:

Activities List:

_____

_____

_____

_____

_____

_____

My favorite foods & drinks:

My best experience today:

Notes & Memories

Photos & Memorabilia

Photos & Memorabilia

Today's Plans:

_____

_____

Cruise Day #_____
Date: ___ / ___ / ___

Places:

Weather:

Activities List:

_____

_____

_____

_____

_____

_____

My favorite foods & drinks:

_____

_____

_____

_____

_____

_____

_____

_____

My best experience today:

_____

_____

_____

_____

_____

_____

_____

_____

Notes & Memories

Photos & Memorabilia

Photos & Memorabilia

Today's Plans:

_____

_____

Cruise Day #_____
Date: ___ / ___ / ___

Places:

Weather:

Activities List:

_____

_____

_____

_____

_____

My favorite foods & drinks:

_____

_____

_____

_____

_____

_____

_____

My best experience today:

_____

_____

_____

_____

_____

_____

Notes &
Memories

Notes & Memories

Photos & Memorabilia

Photos & Memorabilia

Today's Plans:

_____
_____

Cruise Day #_____
Date: ___/___/___

Places:

Weather:

Activities List:
_____
_____
_____
_____
_____
_____

My favorite foods & drinks:

_____
_____
_____
_____
_____
_____
_____
_____
_____
_____

My best experience today:

_____
_____
_____
_____
_____
_____
_____
_____
_____

Notes & Memories

Photos & Memorabilia

Photos & Memorabilia

Today's Plans:
_____
_____

Cruise Day #_____
Date: ___/___/___

Places:

Weather:

Activities List:
_____
_____
_____
_____
_____

My favorite foods & drinks:
_____
_____
_____
_____
_____
_____
_____
_____

My best experience today:
_____
_____
_____
_____
_____
_____
_____

Notes & Memories

Photos & Memorabilia

Photos & Memorabilia

Today's Plans:

_____
_____

Places:

Weather:

Activities List:

_____
_____
_____
_____
_____

My favorite foods & drinks:

_____
_____
_____
_____
_____
_____
_____
_____
_____

My best experience today:

_____
_____
_____
_____
_____
_____
_____

Notes & Memories

Photos & Memorabilia

Photos & Memorabilia

Today's Plans:

_____
_____

Cruise Day #_____
Date: ___/___/___

Places:

Weather:

Activities List:

_____
_____
_____
_____
_____

My favorite foods & drinks:

_____
_____
_____
_____
_____
_____
_____
_____
_____

My best experience today:

_____
_____
_____
_____
_____
_____
_____
_____

Notes & Memories

Notes & Memories

Photos & Memorabilia

Photos & Memorabilia

Today's Plans:

_____

_____

Cruise Day #_____
Date: ___/___/___

Places:

Weather:

Activities List:

_____

_____

_____

_____

_____

_____

My favorite foods & drinks:

_____

_____

_____

_____

_____

_____

_____

_____

_____

My best experience today:

_____

_____

_____

_____

_____

_____

_____

_____

_____

Notes & Memories

Photos & Memorabilia

Photos & Memorabilia

Today's Plans:

_____
_____

Cruise Day #_____
Date: ___/___/___

Places:

Weather:

Activities List:

_____
_____
_____
_____
_____

My favorite foods & drinks:

My best experience today:

Notes & Memories

Photos & Memorabilia

Photos & Memorabilia

Today's Plans:
_____
_____
_____

Cruise Day #_____
Date: ___/___/___

Places:
🌐🏛️🧭🪧

Weather:
☀️🌧️❄️🌡️

Activities List:
📍🏢📷🗺️
_____
_____
_____
_____
_____
_____

My favorite foods & drinks:
_____
_____
_____
_____
_____
_____
_____
_____

My best experience today:
_____
_____
_____
_____
_____
_____
_____
_____

Notes & Memories

Photos & Memorabilia

Photos &
Memorabilia

Today's Plans:

_____
_____

Cruise Day #_____
Date: ___/___/___

Places:

Weather:

Activities List:

_____
_____
_____
_____
_____

My favorite foods & drinks:

_____
_____
_____
_____
_____
_____
_____
_____

My best experience today:

_____
_____
_____
_____
_____
_____
_____
_____

Notes & Memories

Notes & Memories

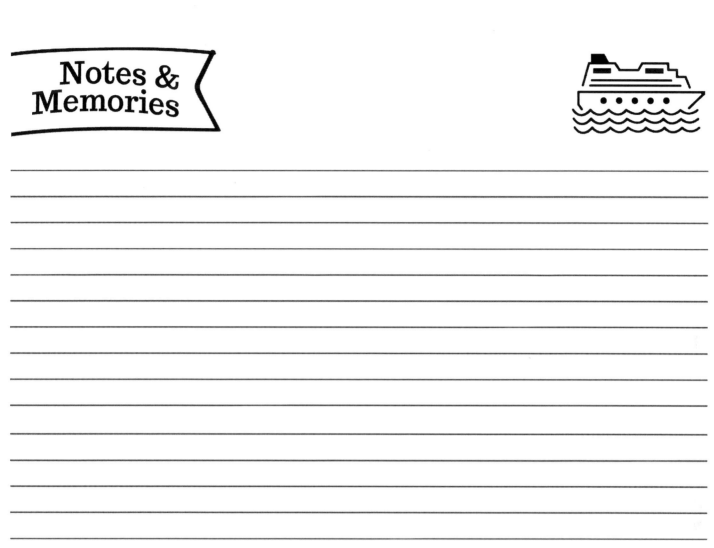

Photos & Memorabilia

Photos & Memorabilia

Today's Plans:

_____
_____

Cruise Day #_____
Date: ___/___/___

Places:

Weather:

Activities List:
_____
_____
_____
_____
_____
_____

My favorite foods & drinks:
_____
_____
_____
_____
_____
_____
_____
_____
_____

My best experience today:
_____
_____
_____
_____
_____
_____
_____
_____

Notes & Memories

Notes & Memories

Photos & Memorabilia

Photos & Memorabilia

Today's Plans:

_____
_____

Cruise Day #_____
Date: ___/___/___

Places:

Weather:

Activities List:
_____
_____
_____
_____
_____

My favorite foods & drinks:

_____
_____
_____
_____
_____
_____
_____
_____

My best experience today:

_____
_____
_____
_____
_____
_____
_____

Notes & Memories

Photos & Memorabilia

Photos & Memorabilia

Today's Plans:

_____
_____

Cruise Day #_____
Date: ___/___/___

Places:

Weather:

Activities List:

_____
_____
_____
_____
_____

My favorite foods & drinks:

My best experience today:

Notes & Memories

Photos & Memorabilia

Photos & Memorabilia

Today's Plans:

_____
_____

Cruise Day #_____
Date: ___/___/___

Places:

Weather:

Activities List:

_____
_____
_____
_____
_____
_____

My favorite foods & drinks:

_____
_____
_____
_____
_____
_____
_____
_____
_____
_____

My best experience today:

_____
_____
_____
_____
_____
_____
_____
_____
_____
_____

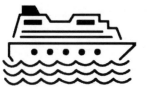

Notes &
Memories

Notes & Memories

Photos & Memorabilia

Photos & Memorabilia

Today's Plans:

_____
_____

Cruise Day #_____
Date: ___/___/___

Places:

Weather:

Activities List:
_____
_____
_____
_____
_____
_____

My favorite foods & drinks:

My best experience today:

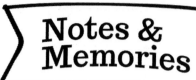

Notes & Memories

Photos & Memorabilia

Photos & Memorabilia

Today's Plans:

_____
_____
_____

Cruise Day #_____
Date: ___/___/___

Places:

Weather:

Activities List:
_____
_____
_____
_____
_____
_____

My favorite foods & drinks:
_____
_____
_____
_____
_____
_____
_____
_____

My best experience today:
_____
_____
_____
_____
_____
_____
_____

Notes & Memories

Notes & Memories

Photos & Memorabilia

Photos & Memorabilia

Today's Plans:

_____

_____

Cruise Day #_____
Date: ___/___/___

Places:

Weather:

Activities List:

_____

_____

_____

_____

_____

_____

My favorite foods & drinks:

_____

_____

_____

_____

_____

_____

_____

_____

_____

My best experience today:

_____

_____

_____

_____

_____

_____

_____

_____

67969007R00063